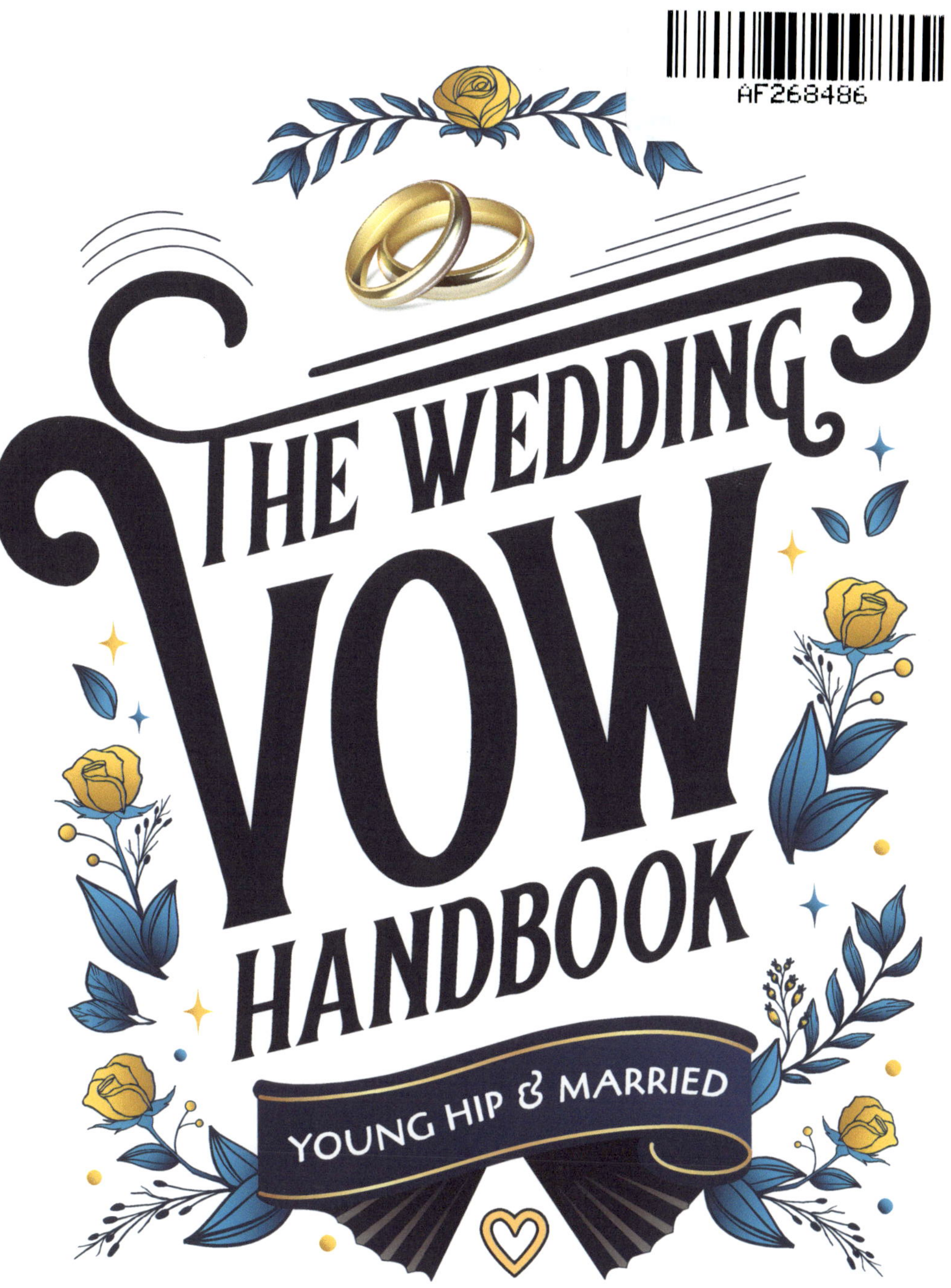

THE WEDDING VOW HANDBOOK

YOUR GUIDE TO CREATING KICK-ASS WEDDING VOWS THAT ARE AUTHENTICALLY YOURS!

SHAWN MILLER

Copyright Page

Dedicated to the love of my life, my wife Erica.

You are the best person I know and the reason I know what love is. Without you this book would not exist.

The Adventure Begins

Welcome to *"The Wedding Vow Handbook: Your Guide to Creating Kick-Ass Wedding Vows That Are Authentically Yours!"* **This book promises to be your ultimate companion on the exciting journey towards crafting heartfelt, unforgettable wedding vows that truly reflect your unique love story.**

If you're a wordsmith, a lover of poetry and flowery language, your vows might be intricate, expressive, and even rhyming. But if you're someone of few words, your vows might be short, sweet, and to the point. Both approaches are equally beautiful and authentic, as long as they come from the heart.

The key to crafting kick-ass wedding vows is staying true to your own voice and letting your love shine through every word, every promise, and every heartfelt sentiment.

In this handbook, you'll be guided through a clear structure that has helped countless couples create their perfect wedding vows. This structure will serve as a foundation, but the content you pour into it will be uniquely yours, as diverse and captivating as your love story.

So, buckle up and get ready for an adventure that will lead you to the heart of what makes truly remarkable wedding vows: the power of love and authenticity.

CONTENTS

The Man Behind the Vows

Hi there! Let me introduce myself: My name is Shawn and I'm the fellow who's going to guide you on this exciting journey towards creating kick-ass, authentic wedding vows. As you might be able to tell, I don't take myself too seriously, but I am incredibly passionate about love, marriage, and the art of crafting heartfelt vows.

I'm a husband, father, and entrepreneur who's fully invested in the wonderful world of weddings. My journey started with my deep passion for marriage and intimate relationships. I believe that these connections are some of the most rewarding experiences we can have in our lives.

That's why I'm dedicated to helping couples not only tie the knot but also thrive in their relationships. Through Young Hip & Married, the company I co-founded with my wife in 2010, I've officiated thousands of weddings and have had the honor of a front row seat at the beginning of so many incredible marriages.

Why Wedding Vows?

As a wedding officiant, I've had the privilege of witnessing countless love stories unfold. I've seen how powerful and transformative wedding vows can be, not just for the couple but also for everyone present at the ceremony. They are the heartbeat of the celebration, a once-in-a-lifetime opportunity for couples to publicly affirm their love and commitment to one another.

Wedding vows are so much more than just a set of promises; they're an expression of the unique love story that brought two people together. When couples write their own vows, they have the chance to honor their beliefs, values, and the essence of who they are as a couple. In my experience, great wedding vows truly make for a great ceremony.

As someone who has officiated over 1500 weddings, I've seen time and time again that the most powerful and memorable wedding vows come straight from the heart. They're deeply personal, genuine, and tailored to who you are as a couple.

So, grab your favorite beverage, get comfortable, and let's dive into this journey together. With this handbook as your guide and a little bit of inspiration, you'll soon have the best wedding vows ever – vows that are authentically yours and brimming with love.

ARE YOU READY?
LET'S GET STARTED!

Deciding on the Big Reveal

One of the first decisions you'll need to make when crafting your kick-ass wedding vows is whether you want to share them with your partner before the big day or keep them as a surprise. Both options have their merits; it ultimately comes down to your personal preferences and the dynamic of your relationship.

Sharing Your Vows Before the Wedding

Some couples prefer to work on their vows together, bouncing ideas off each other and collaborating on their promises. This can be a great bonding experience and ensures that you're both on the same page with the tone and content of your vows.

If you don't like surprises or are worried about getting too emotional during the ceremony, this option might be perfect for you.

Keeping Your Vows a Surprise

For the more adventurous and emotional couples, keeping your vows a surprise can lead to powerful and heartwarming moments during the ceremony. Hearing your partner's vows for the first time as they're being spoken can create an incredibly moving experience that you'll both remember for the rest of your lives.

As a wedding officiant, I'm a little biased towards this option because I've witnessed the beauty of these raw, genuine emotions when couples reveal their vows to one another for the first time. But ultimately, the decision is yours.

So, take a moment to discuss with your partner what feels best for both of you. There's no right or wrong answer – just the one that suits your unique love story. Once you've made your decision, you can move forward with crafting those unforgettable, true to you, wedding vows.

7 Essential Steps

Creating the perfect wedding vows is a journey, and to help guide you on this path, I've developed a 7-step process that has worked wonders for countless couples. In this book, we'll dive deep into each step, ensuring you have all the tools you need to craft kick-ass wedding vows that are authentically yours.

1. OPENING STATEMENT:

The opening statement is crucial for setting the tone of your vows. Don't forget to mention your partner's name as you express your love right from the start.

2. REFLECT:

Take a trip down memory lane and revisit the moments that make up your love story. Reflect on how you fell in love and what brought you to this point in your relationship.

3. COMPLIMENT:

Show your appreciation for your partner by sharing heartfelt compliments. Let them know why they're so special to you and what you love about them.

4. PROMISE:

This is the core of your wedding vows – the promises you make to your partner. Make sure your commitments are meaningful, genuine, and specific to your relationship.

5. KNOW:

What have you learned about your relationship over time? Share the insights, growth, and discoveries that have strengthened your bond.

6. CLOSING STATEMENT:

Wrap up your vows with a heartfelt and powerful closing statement that leaves a lasting impression.

7. DELIVERY:

How you present your vows is just as important as the words you choose. Consider the tone, pacing, and style that best suits your unique love story.

These 7 steps will guide you in crafting the best wedding vows ever, and by the end of this book, you'll have a beautiful, heartfelt expression of your love and commitment to share on your special day.

As you work through the process of creating your wedding vows, keep this spirit of connection alive. Let it guide you and inspire you, helping you to craft heartfelt, authentic vows that truly express the depth of your love.

STEP-1 OPENING STATEMENT:

Set the Tone with Love and Connection

STEP-1: OPENING STATEMENT

Alright, it's time to dive into the opening statement of your wedding vows! Let's kick things off with an opening statement that is personal and heartfelt.

When you begin writing your vows, start with your partner's name. You might think it's obvious, but you'd be surprised how often people forget to address their partner by name when they say their vows.

Of course, it's obvious who you're talking to, but speaking their name aloud in front of your friends and family creates a powerful and intimate moment. This simple act sets the tone for the entire vow exchange.

Next, share how you are feeling in the moment – or how you imagine you'll feel on the big day. Tell them how stunning they look or express your nervous excitement about standing with them at the altar.

1. What specific emotions are you experiencing as you stand in front of your partner? Are you feeling nervous, excited, overwhelmed with love, or a combination of many emotions?

2. How do you want to compliment your partner in your opening statement? Are there any particular attributes or qualities you'd like to highlight, such as their appearance, kindness, or supportiveness?

3. Can you think of a special or memorable moment from your relationship to include in your opening statement? Perhaps it's the moment you first met, a favorite date, or an instance where your partner's actions truly touched your heart.

4. If you want to include humor or lightheartedness in your opening statement, what's a shared joke or funny story that represents your unique connection as a couple?

5. What is the most important message you want to convey to your partner as you begin your vows? Is it a declaration of love, a promise to support and cherish them, or an expression of gratitude for their presence in your life?

Keep in mind that your opening statement is just that, a statement. While you can include a short compliment or reflection about your relationship, we'll dive deeper into those ideas in the following sections of your vows.

Here are a few examples to inspire your own opening statement:

"{Partner's Name}, I stand here today a little nervous and incredibly excited to embark on this journey with you."

"{Partner's Name}, you look absolutely stunning today, and I can't believe the day has finally come for me to marry my best friend."

"{Partner's Name}, who would have thought that when we met, we would be standing here today, about to become spouses?"

"{Partner's Name}, words cannot describe the emotions I'm feeling right now, and I'm the luckiest person in the world to be standing here with you."

Remember, the opening statement sets the tone for your vows. By saying your partner's name, offering a compliment, and sharing your feelings, you create an atmosphere of love, connection, and authenticity.

Don't hesitate to add a touch of lightheartedness or humor if that's more in line with your personality. Just make sure it feels true to who you are as a couple. After all, your wedding vows are a reflection of your unique love story, so let your true selves shine through.

Step-1 TL;DR: Begin your wedding vows with a personal and heartfelt opening statement that includes your partner's name, expresses your emotions, compliments your partner, and sets the tone of love, connection, and authenticity for the rest of your vows.

GOAL: 1 SENTENCE.

Celebrate Your Journey Together

This is where you take a moment to look back on your relationship, reminiscing about how it all began and what you've experienced together. By reflecting on your shared journey, you can emphasize the significance of your wedding day and the love story that brought you both to this moment.

In the Reflect part of your vows, include one or two reflection statements. Think about how you felt when you first met your partner or how they have changed your life for the better. Consider what captivated you about them and how your life has been enriched by having them by your side.

To help you dive into those early days and emotions, you might want to revisit old photos, videos, or journal entries. Reminisce about your first dates, trips, or other shared experiences. This is a chance to highlight the unique aspects of your love story and the emotions that have been a part of your journey.

To help you reminisce about your journey together, consider the following questions:

1. What was the moment you realized you were in love with your partner? How did it feel, and how did it change your perspective on life and relationships?

2. What is your favorite memory or shared experience with your partner, and why is it so significant to your relationship?

3. How has your partner supported and encouraged you during challenging times? Share an example of when their love and support made a difference in your life.

4. What qualities or traits do you most admire in your partner, and how have they made a positive impact on your life?

5. In what ways has your relationship with your partner grown or evolved over time? How have you both changed as individuals and as a couple since you first met?

Here are some example reflection statements to inspire your own:

- "From the moment our paths crossed, you've surprised, captivated, and challenged me in ways I never knew were possible. I've fallen in love with you again and again, and I still can't believe I get to marry you."

- "From the moment I saw you, I knew you were someone I had to get to know. Little did I know that we would be standing here today, ready to become a married couple."

- "We've been through so much together - not all of it easy – but together, we have made it through every challenge life has thrown at us."

- "Before I knew you, I had no idea what love really was. Thank you for taking a chance on me and helping me become the person I am today."

Feel free to borrow, modify, or mix and match any of these examples to create a reflection statement that feels authentic to your love story. Remember, your vows are a celebration of your unique journey together, so let your shared experiences and emotions lead your writing.

Step-2 TL;DR: Reflect on your journey together by reminiscing about significant moments, expressing how your partner has impacted your life, and highlighting the growth and positive qualities in your relationship, crafting a reflection statement that celebrates your unique love story.

GOAL: 1-2 SENTENCES

Shower Your Partner with Praise

The complimenting phase of your wedding vows is an opportunity to make your partner blush with heartfelt praise. This section is a favorite for many, as it allows you to genuinely express your admiration and appreciation for your partner in front of the people who mean the most to both of you.

In this part of your vows, shower your partner with genuine compliments. Don't hold anything back! Share the qualities, characteristics, and actions that you truly adore about your partner. Imagine that you're the only two people in the room and share your thoughts as if it were just the two of you.

When crafting your compliments, think about who your partner is, what they work hard at, and how they've helped your relationship flourish or how they've helped you grow. Consider the qualities that others recognize in them and the traits they've developed over time.

1. What are the top three qualities or characteristics that you most admire in your partner? Consider the traits that make them unique and why they are so important to you.

2. Can you recall a moment or specific event where your partner demonstrated one of these admirable qualities? How did it make you feel and what did you learn about them in that moment?

3. How has your partner helped you grow as an individual, both emotionally and in other aspects of your life? What specific actions or support have they provided that you are most grateful for?

4. How do others (friends, family, or colleagues) perceive your partner? What positive qualities do they often mention or praise, and do you share the same admiration for those qualities?

5. Think about your partner's passions, talents, or hobbies. How do these aspects of their life inspire you or make you feel proud to be their partner?

Here are some example compliments to inspire your own:

- "You are the most beautiful, stunning, and radiant person I've ever laid eyes on."

- "I've never met anyone as kind and compassionate as you. Your kindness truly touches everyone around you."

- "Your patience and understanding have allowed me to grow beyond anything I could have ever imagined."

- "When I look into your eyes, all my worries and troubles fade away. It's like you hold magic in your eyes."

- "Your love for your family is an inspiration to me, and I'm grateful to be a part of it."

Feel free to borrow, modify, or mix and match any of these examples to create compliments that genuinely reflect your feelings for your partner. Remember, your vows are a celebration of your unique love story, so share your heartfelt admiration for your partner.

Step-3 TL;DR: Use this phase of your vows to sincerely compliment your partner, expressing admiration for their qualities, actions, and impact on your life, and celebrating their unique attributes in front of your loved ones.

GOAL: 2 SENTENCES

STEP-4 PROMISE:

Your Commitments and Visions for the Future

The promising stage is typically what people think of when they think of wedding vows. This section is where you make 2-4 promise statements about what you commit to, who you want to be, and what you envision for your future together. You can interchange the words "promise," "vow," and "I will" to keep things varied and interesting.

This section is the heart of your vows and should include promises about your character, the things you want to create together as a couple, and how you want to behave in your marriage. Consider your personal growth, your relationship dynamics, and your aspirations for your life together.

1. What are the core values and principles that you want to uphold and nurture in your relationship? Consider the qualities that are most important to you and your partner.

2. Reflect on the ways you can support your partner's personal growth and dreams. What specific actions or behaviors can you commit to that will help them achieve their goals?

3. How can you contribute to creating a strong and lasting bond with your partner? Consider the aspects of your relationship that require nurturing, patience, or understanding, and how you can commit to addressing them.

4. What are some challenges that you and your partner may face together in the future? How can you commit to facing these obstacles as a team and working through them with love and compassion?

5. Think about the moments and experiences you want to share with your partner in your life together. What promises can you make to ensure that you both continue to grow, learn, and enjoy your time together?

Here are some example promise statements to inspire your own:

- "I will always remind you how awesome you are, inside and out, at least once a day, especially when you're not believing it yourself."

- "I promise to remain true to myself and continue to grow as an individual and as your partner."

- "I know I will likely frustrate you and challenge you, but I'll do my best to work on the things I know bother you."

- "I will be open and honest with you in all things and communicate my needs and feelings in a way you can understand."

- "I promise to support and protect your freedom, respecting your individuality and continuing to seek a deep understanding of your wishes, desires, fears, and dreams."

- "I vow to respect, admire, and appreciate you for who you are, as well as for the person you wish to become, and to meet your needs not out of obligation, but because it delights me to see you happy."

- I promise to take care of myself to the best of my ability so that I can remain healthy and grow old by your side

- "I promise to work together to keep our lives exciting, adventurous, and full of passion, persevering when times get tough, and conquering challenges together."

Feel free to borrow, modify, or mix and match any of these examples to create promise statements that genuinely reflect your commitment to your partner and your vision for your future together. Remember, your vows are an expression of your unique love story, so the promises you make to one another should be unique to you two.

Step-4 TL;DR: In the promise stage of your vows, make promise statements that reflect your commitment to upholding core values, supporting personal growth, addressing challenges together, and creating a fulfilling future as a couple.

GOAL: 3 SENTENCES

Express Your Certainty and Belief in Your Relationship

The knowing section is a powerful way to wrap up your wedding vows. In this section, you'll choose one knowing statement that captures the essence of your certainty and belief in your relationship.

This statement serves as a powerful affirmation of your commitment and the strength of your love. By expressing your confidence in your partnership, you are also re-assuring your partner of the strength and resilience of your marital bond.

To create a knowing statement that resonates with you and your partner, consider the following questions:

1. What are the key elements of your relationship that give you confidence in your future together?

2. How have you and your partner overcome challenges in the past, and what does that say about your ability to face whatever may come your way?

3. What are the unique aspects of your relationship that make you believe you can weather any storm and come out stronger on the other side?

4. How do you envision your love evolving and growing stronger over time?

5. In what ways do you see your partnership as a source of strength and support, not just for each other, but also for those around you?

Reflecting on these questions can help you craft a knowing statement that captures your unwavering belief in your relationship's resilience and the love you share. It should reinforce the commitment you've made to each other and the enduring love that will carry you through your life together.

Here are some example knowing statements to inspire your own:

- "I know that no matter what happens, we're going to work it out together."

- "I know that I will love you until my last breath."

- "I know that no matter how much time has passed, our love will never fade, and we will continue to grow side by side."

- "I believe in the truth of what we are and that we were made for each other."

- "I know that whatever life throws our way, we will accomplish it together."

- "I know that year after year, and wrinkle after wrinkle, our love will only become stronger."

- "I know life will not always be easy, but together, we can make the difficult times a lot more fun."

- "I know that our love will continue to be a guiding light, illuminating our path and leading us through life's most incredible adventures."

Feel free to borrow, modify, or mix and match any of these examples to create your own knowing statement that genuinely reflects your certainty and belief in your relationship. Remember, your vows are an authentic celebration of your relationship, and this statement serves as the powerful conclusion to the promises you're making to one another.

Step-5 TL;DR: In the knowing section, choose a powerful knowing statement that affirms your unwavering belief in your relationship's resilience, enduring love, and ability to face any challenge together, serving as a strong conclusion to your vows.

GOAL: 1 SENTENCE

Summarize and Reaffirm Your Commitment

The closing statement is your opportunity to encapsulate all of the promises, compliments, reflections, and knowing statements you've made in your vows in a short conclusion, while reasserting your commitment to your partner.

This is a simple but powerful way to wrap up your vows, leaving a lasting impression on your partner and your guests. Without a closing statement, it can feel like your vows end abruptly or like you might continue on. Instead, choose or create a closing statement that ties a bow on your vows, genuinely reflecting your feelings and the essence of your relationship.

1. What message do you want to leave your partner with as you conclude your vows? Reflect on the overarching theme of your vows and the emotions you want to convey.

2. How can you best express the depth of your love and commitment to your partner in just a few words? Think about the language that best captures the essence of your bond.

3. What aspects of your relationship do you want to highlight as you bring your vows to a close? Consider the unique and special qualities of your partnership.

4. How can your closing statement create a sense of continuity and connection to the promises and sentiments you've shared throughout your vows?

5. What emotions do you want your closing statement to evoke in your partner and your guests? Reflect on the feelings you want to leave them with as you conclude your vows.

Here are some example closing statements to inspire your own:

- "This is my promise now and forever."

- "This is my sacred vow."

- "I will love you from this moment until my last."

- "My love for you will never fade."

- "Loving you is the best thing that ever happened to me, and I can't wait to spend the rest of my life with you."

- "You have my heart and my soul."

- "My heart belongs to you now and forever."

- "You are truly my soulmate, and I will be with you forever."

- "Words cannot describe how I feel, so I will simply say I love you, always have, and always will."

- "From this day forward, I pledge my love, my life, and my heart to you."

Feel free to borrow, modify, or mix and match any of these examples to create your own closing statement that feels authentic to the two of you. Take your time to choose or create a closing statement that resonates with you both. This statement will be the final touch on your wedding vows, serving as a heartfelt reminder of the love and commitment you share.

Once you have your closing statement, review your vows as a whole to ensure they flow smoothly and authentically represent your feelings and promises to one another.

Step-6 TL;DR: In the closing statement, choose or create a concise and heartfelt statement that summarizes and reaffirms your commitment, leaving a lasting impression and tying a bow on your vows while reflecting the essence of your relationship.

GOAL: 1-2 SENTENCE

Tips for Presenting Your Wedding Vows

When the time comes to share your vows with one another, trust me, you're going to be swept away by a tidal wave of emotions, feelings you've never experienced before. So, it's absolutely crucial to start with a solid foundation of connection.

Connection is all about being present in the moment, feeling grounded and centered, and truly embracing the love you share with your partner.

I can't stress this enough: connection is key. So many people get caught up in the whirlwind of emotions, they forget to take that essential moment to connect with their partner. Remember, you're in this together – so, make sure you're there for each other, heart and soul, every step of the way.

It's now time to think about how you want to deliver your vows to each other. The way you present your vows can greatly impact the emotional impact of the ceremony.

Here are the five different ways to share your vows:

1. YOUR OFFICIANT READS THE VOWS AND YOU SAY I DO:

With this option, your wedding officiant will read your vows out loud and you will answer by saying, "I do." This delivery style works best if you're nervous about reading your own vows, but can be a bit awkward as your officiant will read your personal words.

2. YOUR OFFICIANT READS THE VOWS, ONE LINE AT A TIME, AS YOU REPEAT THEM:

Repeat-after-me wedding vows allow you to say your own vows, but with the support of your officiant. This delivery style is best suited to shorter vows, as they'll be said four times (your officiant, you repeating, your officiant again, your partner repeating).

3. YOU READ YOUR OWN WEDDING VOWS:

This vow delivery style is the most personal and, often, most preferable for guests (and couples!). In this style, you will simply read your own wedding vows to your partner like a letter. After all, who better to deliver the vows you wrote than you?

BONUS: 3. Since your officiant isn't needed, they can step to the side and allow you to have a personal moment with your spouse-to-be.

4. YOU MEMORIZE YOUR WEDDING VOWS:

Memorizing your wedding vows (or worse, making them up on the spot!) may seem romantic in the movies but is far from it in real life. Memorizing your vows can be challenging, especially with the emotions of the day, and you might get flustered or forget your lines.

5. YOU SHARE YOUR WEDDING VOWS IN PRIVATE:

Instead of sharing your vows in front of all of your guests, you may opt for a personal moment, sharing them in private before the ceremony. While this can be more intimate and less nerve wracking, you do miss out on making a powerful, public declaration of love and commitment to your partner.

I believe there's something magical about writing and reading your own words to your partner in front of all of your loved ones, but there's no one right way to deliver your vows. Discuss the options above with your partner and decide what works best for both of you.

Here are some tips to ensure a successful delivery of your wedding vows:

1. DON'T RUSH:

Give yourselves a moment to genuinely connect with each other before you share your vows. Lock eyes, hold hands if you can, and take a deep breath together. Then, once you feel grounded and present, begin your vows.

2. DECIDE WHO GOES FIRST:

Determine the order of vow delivery. It's often a good idea for the person who is more likely to cry to go first.

3. HAVE YOUR OFFICIANT HOLD YOUR VOWS:

To make it easier on yourself, ask your officiant to hold your vows during the ceremony. This will prevent you from having to dig through your clothing to find them.

4. USE A MICROPHONE:

Even if it's an intimate ceremony, consider using a microphone. It can be hard to project your voice when you're emotional, and a microphone ensures everyone can hear your vows clearly.

5. PRACTICE YOUR VOWS:

Familiarize yourself with your vows by reading them multiple times before the ceremony. Keep them in a notes folder on your phone and review them whenever you have a spare moment. Make sure you also practice saying them out loud, ideally in front of a mirror, so you can get a feel for how the words sound coming out of your mouth.

6. PRINT OR WRITE YOUR VOWS:

Have your vows printed or neatly written out on a small piece of paper or vow book. Avoid using your phone to read your vows as it can look tacky and be distracting.

7. EDIT YOUR VOWS FOR EASY READING:

Make sure your vows are formatted in a way that makes them easy to read during the ceremony.

By following these tips, you can deliver your wedding vows confidently and ensure that your ceremony is a beautiful, memorable experience for you, your partner, and your guests.

Sample Wedding Vows

OPENING STATEMENT:

{Partner's Name},

I stand here today, in awe of your beauty, grace and charm

a little nervous and very excited, because today I finally get to call you my partner for life.

REFLECT:

When we first met I had no idea I had just met my best friend and the love of my life.

Little did I know all the incredible Adventures that awaited me with you as my partner.

COMPLIMENT:

You are the most beautiful, stunning, and radiant person I've ever laid eyes on.

Your capacity for love and acceptance is beyond anything I have ever known, not a day goes by where you don't amaze me in some way.

PROMISE:

I promise to always do my best and to challenge you to grow.

I will encourage you when you're down and push you even when you think you can't make it, but I know you can.

I will never criticize you to others and I will always speak my heart to you honestly, even when it scares me to do so.

KNOW:

I know life will throw us challenges, but I will never leave your side, no matter how hard it gets.

CLOSING STATEMENT:

Never forget that I'm your greatest fan, and I love you more than words can say.

And will continue to do so until my very last breath.

Thank you!

As we reach the end of this book, I want to take a moment to express my heartfelt gratitude and appreciation to each and every one of you who has taken the time to read it.

I hope that the contents of this book have provided you with valuable guidance and inspiration as you embark on your journey of love and commitment with your partner. It has been a privilege to be a part of your story, and I am deeply grateful for the opportunity to have made a difference in your lives.

I wish you and your partner a lifetime of love, happiness, and growth together. May your bond strengthen with each passing day, and may you continue to find joy in each other's company.

Thank you once again for choosing to embark on this vow writing journey with me. It has been an absolute pleasure, please know that I'm in your corner cheering you as you share your vows with your partner.

Wishing you all the love and happiness your hearts can hold,

SHAWN